How Are You Today?

A CELEBRATION OF CHILDREN'S EMOTIONS

By Linda M. Mitchell

OMNIPIX BOOKS

omnipixbooks.com

How Are You Today?
A Celebration of Children's Emotions

ISBN (paperback): 978-0-9856695-6-0
ISBN (eBook): 978-0-9856695-7-7

Published by
Omnipix Books
omnipixbooks.com

┌─── **Photographs of children's emotions** ───┐

— By Odell Mitchell Jr. —
Boisterous, bored, eager, feisty, friendly, grown-up, happy, nervous, nurturing,
playful, satisfied, scared, shy, sick, smart, special, sweet, tense, upset, and zany.

— From depositphotos.com —
Athletic @miladamova/Lyudmila Adamova, brave @MiMaLeFi/Mariia Siurtukova,
competitive @vectorfusionart/Sean Prior, excited @boggy22/Goran Bogicevic,
fascinated @parinyabinsuk/Parinya Binsuk, helpful @ zurijeta/Jasmin Merdan,
mischievous @Gelpi/José Manuel Gelpi Díaz, quiet @Reanas/Elena Stepanova,
sad @DimaKozitsyn/Dima Kozitsyn, silly @Cherry-Merry/Tatyana Chernyak,
talented @londondeposit/Craig Robinson.

— Image credits —
Emojis from depositphotos.com: @pingebat/Roberto Scandola, @YummyBuum/
Olga Kurbatova, @SpicyTruffel/Roman Egorov. Cover backround texture from
adobestock.com/EnginKorkmaz.

Editing and proofreading: Misti Moyer

Design by Monica Thomas for TLC Book Design,
TLCBookDesign.com

Printed in the United States of America

*For my husband, who never put the camera
down and captured real life moments.*

*And for all the children who make us laugh,
smile and sometimes cry.*

—L.M.M.

I'M FEELING
ATHLETIC.

What sports do you play?

I'M FEELING
BOISTEROUS.

 When are you loud
and full of energy?

I'M FEELING
BORED.

When have you
felt bored?

I'M FEELING
BRAVE.

What have you done
that is brave?

I'M FEELING COMPETITIVE.

How do you feel when
you win or lose?

I'M FEELING EAGER.

What do you want
to do today?

I'M FEELING EXCITED.

What makes you
feel excited?

I'M FEELING
FASCINATED.

What is fascinating to you?

I'M FEELING
FEISTY.

When have you
felt feisty?

I'M FEELING
FRIENDLY.

Who are your
friends?

I'M FEELING
GROWN-UP.

When have you
felt grown-up?

I'M FEELING
HAPPY.

What makes
you happy?

I'M FEELING
HELPFUL.

How do you
help others?

I'M FEELING
MISCHIEVOUS.

How do you get
into mischief?

I'M FEELING
NERVOUS.

What makes you
feel nervous?

I'M FEELING
NURTURING.

What do you
nurture?

I'M FEELING PLAYFUL.

What do you do
when you play?

I'M FEELING
QUIET.

When do you
get quiet?

I'M FEELING
SAD.

What makes
you sad?

I'M FEELING
SATISFIED.

When do you
feel satisfied?

I'M FEELING SCARED.

What makes you
feel scared?

I'M FEELING SHY.

When have you felt shy?

I'M FEELING SICK.

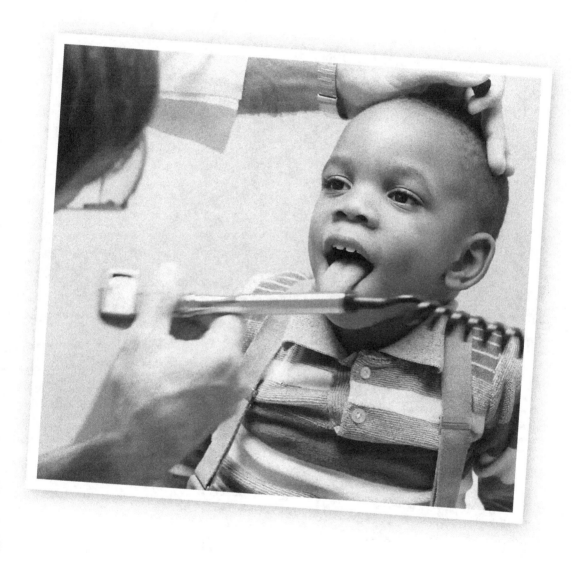

What happens when
you feel sick?

I'M FEELING
SILLY.

What have you done
that was silly?

I'M FEELING
SMART.

When do you
feel smart?

I'M FEELING
SPECIAL.

What makes you feel special?

I'M FEELING
SWEET.

When have you
felt sweet?

I'M FEELING
TALENTED.

What talents do
you have?

I'M FEELING
TENSE.

What makes you
feel tense?

I'M FEELING
UPSET.

When do you feel upset?

I'M FEELING
ZANY.

When have you felt zany?

Vocabulary

ATHLETIC: active in sports or exercises

BOISTEROUS: full of energy; exuberant; noisy

BORED: uninterested

BRAVE: to face or handle despite being afraid; courageous

COMPETITIVE: having a strong desire to win or be more successful than others

EAGER: feeling a strong and impatient desire to do something

EXCITED: very enthusiastic and eager

FASCINATED: finding something interesting; curiosity

FEISTY: spunky; energetic; not afraid to fight or argue

FRIENDLY: showing the kindness and warmth of a friend; being other than an enemy

GROWN-UP: no longer young; like an adult; mature

HAPPY: being pleased or glad

HELPFUL: giving help

MISCHIEVOUS: playful in a naughty or teasing way

NERVOUS: having uncomfortable feelings; easily excited; jumpy

NURTURING: giving nourishment or tender care

PLAYFUL: showing that you are having fun and not being serious

QUIET: making little or no noise; calm

SAD: feeling or showing unhappiness, grief or sorrow

SATISFIED: being pleased; content

SCARED: feeling afraid

SHY: not feeling comfortable meeting and talking to people; easily frightened

SICK: not feeling well

SILLY: playful and lighthearted; not serious; foolish

SMART: quick to learn or do; mentally alert; bright; clever

SPECIAL: feeling liked a lot; unusual and better in some way

SWEET: very gentle, kind or friendly

TALENTED: having ability and skill to do something well

TENSE: not relaxed; feeling or showing worry or nervousness

UPSET: angry; distressed; unhappy

ZANY: clownish; wacky; fantastically crazy

Discussion Guide

The following activities will help children explore their own thoughts and ideas about the emotions shown by the children in the book.

1. Can you relate to the emotions in this photo?

   Tell or write about a time you felt this way.

2. Can you describe some other moods and feelings you think are shown in the picture?

3. Can you change the descriptive word for the picture to another form? For example, "happy," "happier," "happiest."

4. Finish the sentence:

   The picture I like best is _____, because...

5. Can you draw a picture of one of the emotions? Or, can you take a photograph of someone expressing an emotion?

About the author Linda M. Mitchell

Linda M. Mitchell is a former teacher and the founder and executive director of the Metro East Literacy Project nonprofit organization.

Look for Linda's other books in the Photographic Celebration Series at LindaMitchellBooks.com

PHOTO BY ODELL MITCHELL JR.

Thank you to featured photographer Odell Mitchell Jr.

PHOTO BY TIM PARKER

Odell Mitchell Jr. is a former photographer for the *St. Louis Post-Dispatch*. He is a Missouri Photojournalism Hall of Fame inductee whose award-winning photos have been published in national magazines, books and exhibits.

CPSIA information can be obtained
at www.ICGtesting.com
Printed in the USA
JSHW042019201220
10393JS00002B/62